C000271974

Anne-Katrin Hagen

The Structured Schooling of Horses

Foundations of Success

CADMOS
EQUESTRIAN

Contents

Imprint

Copyright of original edition ©2002 by Cadmos Verlag GmbH, Brunsbek.
Copyright for this edition
©2003 by Cadmos Verlag GmbH, Brunsbek.
Translated by: Claire Williams
Project Management: Editmaster Co. Ltd, Northampton.
Design and setting: Ravenstein + Partner, Verden.
Photographs: Angelika Schmelzer
Printed by Proost, Turnhout
All rights reserved
Copying or storage in electronic media is permitted only
with the prior written permission of the publishers.

Printed in Belgium

ISBN 3-86127-937-1

Introduction

Training your own horse can be a fascinating exercise, but only a rider with a correct and independent seat, and a good drop of courage, should take on this task. Young horses are sometimes rather full of the joys of life!

The rider should have gathered as much experience as possible from many types of horse. A rider who takes on the training of a young horse should themselves have had a good foundation of training.

You always need to bear in mind that the horse is one of the noblest animals in creation. It is both an animal of flight and a herd

The dominant mare is the first to the trough and is first through the gate when it's time to go in. When the leader of the herd comes, all the others make way.

horse. Despite our love of the horse and its beauty, the horse is still a horse – it thinks, feels and behaves like a horse, and the handler must always remember that!

The Golden Rule: An inexperienced horse needs an experienced rider and an inexperienced rider needs an experienced horse!

animal. The instinct for flight still exists in domestic horses, slightly stronger in some than in others. Even with discipline, this instinct can never be entirely overcome. This can only be achieved through the building of trust.

A strict hierarchy exists in herds, and the leader (usually a mare) is respected by all the rest. For the rider who takes on the training of a young horse, this means that he must take on the role of the herd leader. From the start the rider must therefore earn respect and build up trust. Beware of humanising the

The Aim of training

At the end of a systematic training programme (lasting at least two years), the horse should have become more appealing to the eye: it will have developed muscles in the right places, its movement will be free and supple, and its presence and expressiveness will have developed. The horse will respond to finely tuned, barely perceptible aids and instructions. It will allow itself to be bent and flexed and ridden forwards in the required outline at a rhythmic, loose and even pace. The hindquarters will carry more weight so that the forehand becomes freer in its movement. It will go through water without any problems and will be able to

tackle small jumps. Full of trust – for the horse is certain that it will never be over-faced by its rider – it will be happy out hacking, in the school and on the road. In short: it will be "pleasant to ride".

The path to this goal is long, and demands discipline, perseverance and endless patience. The only way to achieve this is through a sensible plan of small steps, one building on the next. Any short cut or deviation from this path ("Tips and Tricks…" or " The expert says…") will lead unmistakably in the wrong direction. It takes much longer to fill gaps in training or to correct mistakes. Often the results of such errors cannot be rectified and the horse will be a physical or mental wreck for its all too often short life.

Some basic systems of training

In the early 1950s the German Equestrian Federation developed the "Principles of Riding and Driving". These principles talked about the "Training Scale" for the first time. They were based on Gustav Steinbrecht's (1808 – 1886) *Gymnasium" des Pferdes* (Gymnasium of the Horse) with the guiding principle: " Ride your horse forwards and straight!" Steinbrecht's classic was first published (posthumously) in 1886, and from it Hans von Heydebrecht (1866 – 1935) and a committee then developed the military service regulations, for cavalry training in the German army. This training system is still unaltered today as the basis for all official training manuals of the German Equestrian Federation.

In the meantime, though, half a century

has passed. The experience from working with young horses and the changing demands of today's equestrian sport have made it necessary to rethink and expand the "Training Scale". Kurd Albrecht von Ziegner, born in 1918, cavalry officer and highly successful in show jumping and dressage, took part in the reworking of the Federation's training system. He had been involved with the training of young horses to the highest level and had given much thought to the most sensible and careful way to reach this point. He extended the German Federation's Training Scale by four points and slightly altered the order of the individual steps. Thus a logical concept of "small steps", or "Elements", emerged, that made the systematic development from basic to advanced movements possible.

Both training concepts consist of three large blocks. The first block is the *familiarisation phase*, in which the horse is given a basic education (tying up, lifting the feet, getting used to being rugged up, saddled and bridled) and learns to be worked on the lunge. Being backed is a very profound experience for the young horse. If it is not done with a lot of patience, sensitivity and knowledge, then serious mistakes can be made at this early stage. The same applies to lungeing. Much damage can be done to the horse's ability to move well as a result of incorrect lungeing. Under a rider; the horse learns to move in a *loose* and *relaxed, rhythmical* way, with ground covering paces (*freedom*) through a light connection to the rider's hand (contact). The second block is the *development of forward thrust*. It is inter-linked

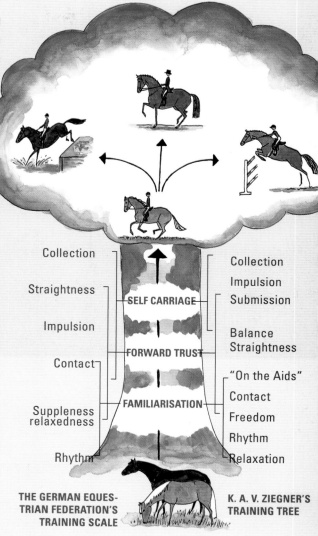

Collection

Straightness

Impulsion

Contact

Suppleness relaxedness

Rhythm

SELF CARRIAGE

FORWARD TRUST

FAMILIARISATION

Collection

Impulsion

Submission

Balance
Straightness

"On the Aids"

Contact

Freedom

Rhythm

Relaxation

**THE GERMAN EQUES-
TRIAN FEDERATION'S
TRAINING SCALE**

**K. A. V. ZIEGNER'S
TRAINING TREE**

to the first block. For the horse to develop forward thrust from the hindquarters, it must have established a secure contact with the rider's hand and must work comfortably *on the aids*. More and more attention can then be given to *straightness;* and as a result the horse will become more balanced, meaning that it will learn to move with the hind legs following the path of the front legs in circles and turns.

Only a relaxed horse can learn.

The third block is *the development of self-carriage*. At this stage, the points of the preceding blocks must be well established: once the horse has found its lateral *balance,* (it is easily flexed and bent); it needs to develop its longitudinal balance, i.e. from the back to the front. The horse moves its centre of gravity more under itself and puts more weight on its haunches. That is only possible when the horse is *coming through* more (known in Germany as *Durchlässigkeit*). The horse is capable of good transitions and is "comfortable to ride". From these transitions, also within the paces, emerges *impulsion*. At the moment when the forward impulsion of a supple horse is captured and contained and the horse engages its hocks more, *collection* is achieved, with the related raising of the forehand. The hindquarters come more under the horse, the croup lowers and the forehand lifts. The paces become more elevated.

In principle, the two training systems are similar. The biggest difference lies in the fact that in the training tree, impulsion lies more towards the top of the scale. However since all the elements merge into each other, this is more easily understood.

In the German Federation's training system, all of the individual points taken together produce submission. At first glance that is logical. But without treating submission as a separate and important element that needs to be constantly worked on, then impulsion and therefore collection cannot be developed,

Relaxednes and Suppleness

Relaxedness is the most important element of a young horse's education and the foundation of all further training. Also included under this term is calmness, trust and contentment.

A relaxed horse moves with a swinging, rounded back. The neck has enough room to stretch, the horse looks content and there is a line of foam around the lips. Its paces are even and regular and if on top of this the horse also gently snorts, then the rider should be satisfied – the horse is happy in its work. The reason why relaxedness is so important throughout training, up to the highest levels, can be better understood when looking at the horse's skeleton and its two main muscle groups.

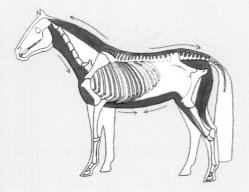

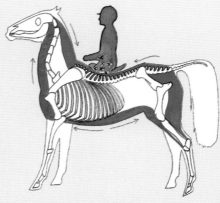

The top group of muscles begins at the poll, running down both sides of the crest of the neck along the back, widening over the croup and down to the hocks.
The muscles on the sides of the crest are especially important (note the narrow chain of the cervical or neck vertebra in the much thicker neck), because they pull the spine in the back region upwards, i.e. the vertebrae apart, when the neck is flexing forwards and downwards.
The lower muscle group begins in the throat area, runs down underneath the neck and extends from the chest along the entire abdominal wall over the stifle and the thigh to the hock.

The young horse tenses the top muscle group as soon as it feels a rider's weight. Since the back muscles are connected to both the neck and the croup muscles, the neck will be pulled upwards and the haunches will be pushed out and back.
The stomach muscles on the other hand will be relaxed and as a result the back will sag. The vertebrae of the spine along the back will come dangerously close to touching each other. If this isn't stopped by suitable gymnastic exercises, then it can lead to the particularly painful "kissing spines syndrome".

A muscle can only contract; in order to relax again, it needs an opposing muscle. In contracting, the muscle uses energy, in this case oxygen, and in relaxing it recovers because it is then supplied with blood and thus receives new oxygen.

If a muscle stays contracted over a longer period of time, there is no rest phase and no new oxygen reaching it. The result is tenseness, which can escalate into painful cramps.

Resting the muscle requires a tightening of the opposing muscle group. For instance, in order to achieve relaxation of the upper muscle groups, stretching the neck helps greatly. This will lead to a healthier horse and to a longer working life at higher levels of performance

How is relaxedness achieved?

On the lunge, the young horse will have already learned to go in a relaxed manner in the three basic paces. By placing a rider on its back, however, everything is instantly

Experience is vital here! Young horses learn fast.

When riding in the forward seat, shorten the stirrups by two or three holes.

its ribs – the poor animal will be completery tensed up. Many young horses try to get rid of this new burden by bucking. Much experience and empathy is required from the rider, and this is no job for the anxious or inexperienced. In the first months of basic training it is a great challenge for a trainer to reproduce the same state of relaxation achieved on the lunge under the new burden of a rider and to establish the regularity of its natural paces. This phase of training requires time; there are no shortcuts. The amount of time that is required will depend on the individual horse's conformation and nerves and disposition, as well as on the rider's ability. If you hurry through this stage however, it can cause irreversible damage to the horse.

changed. Weight on its back, a person above its head, the unfamiliar feel of a leg against

Pole work is the best way to start. The young horse learns to look where it is going and finds its own rhythm.

When riding uphill, the horse's nose should be allowed forward. The hindquarters push through from behind and the horse will stretch into a longer outline.

The next stage is work over cavaletti. Both exercises strengthen the horse's back.

When riding downhill the hind legs will tread more underneath the horse and the head will go onto the vertical – the horse is in effect rounding up into more of a collected outline.

Initially, ride with a forward or light seat so you can feather your own weight through the upper leg. It makes most sense to start with large circles, as the horse will be familiar with this work from lungeing. In addition, it's easier for the horse to take off on you on long straight lines!

If the horse can work with its neck and back swinging, moving forward calmly and trusting with even paces, then it will gradually work onto the bit and take up a contact with the hand. Now would be the time to try a sitting trot for a short time. When transitioning from rising to sitting trot, the knees should be held firmly against the saddle in order to absorb the rider's weight. Here too sensitivity is called for – does the horse take your full weight without losing rhythm or tensing its back? If this is not the case go to a rising trot and try it again. As a reward, let the horse take the rein down so its back can stretch. This applies throughout the entire training process. If additional skills are required, then work can be started on pole and cavaletti work in all paces. Hacking out up and down hills also adds variety into the daily routine and is a wonderful method of building muscles that will be required by the horse in the future. In addition it helps to develop elasticity and surefootedness, as well as building up trust between horse and rider.

Rhythm

Relaxedness and rhythm are inseparable. If the horse is not relaxed; it can't move with regularity and rhythm. Every horse has its own natural rhythm when relaxed. This rhythm depends, among other things, on the horse's conformation, but in all cases the horse should be worked in its own rhythm. Each pace has its own natural rhythm – the walk is four-beat, the trot two-beat and the canter three-beat. Sometimes the rhythm and regularity of the pace may not be true – a walk may become almost a two-beat rhythm and the canter a four– beat. Both are major faults. The rider should always take care to ride an even and clear rhythm. This also depends on the seat and effectiveness of the rider: anyone without an independent seat will not be able to feel the movement of his horse.

The basic paces and variations within paces

There are three basic paces – walk, trot and canter. In each pace a number of tempos can be ridden. Apart from the working tempo – the pace at which a young horse finds it easiest to find its balance – there are the collected, medium and extended paces. In the walk there are just collected, medium and extended.

You can easily feel and count the phases of the walk.

The walk has four beats or steps, with the horse placing its feet one after the other – left hind, left fore, right hind, right fore. There is no moment of suspension, which makes the walk a gait without impulsion. It should be purposeful and forward-going, but not hurried. The horse should move forward in a calm and relaxed manner, be straight and have an even contact on both reins. The four beats should be able to be clearly counted: 1-2-3-4 and so on. If the well defined four beats are lost (1-2, 3-4), the walk is incorrect. When only two beats are heard the horse is pacing – a major fault. The medium walk is the only one used with the young horse; the collected walk where the hindquarters step more under the body, as well as the extended walk where the steps are longer, are only ridden in the higher levels of dressage.

In order to keep the walk correct, it is important for the back and poll to stay relaxed. The horse should be allowed to stretch slightly forward and downwards and the rider's hand should softly follow the natural to-and-fro movement of the horse's head. The best way to do this is by riding circles, but never ride in walk for too long. Trot or canter for a while, then come back to the walk in between. The walk is the only pace that can be ruined by doing too much of it, so be careful! Walking on a a long rein though allows both horse and rider to recover from hard work.

Trot

The trot has two beats. The horse uses diagonal pairs of legs alternately (right hind/left fore and left hind/right fore). In between, there is a moment of suspension that can

In trot, counting the beats is very easy.

make it full of impulsion. There are four different forms of trot – collected, working, medium and extended. When starting dressage the working trot is used as well as "lengthening strides", which leads to medium trot. The working trot should be ridden in an active, forward way, with the horse swinging along rhythmically on a soft contact. The tempo must be such that the horse does not lose rhythm in the turns or when changing reins. To protect the young horse's back, it is best to rise to the trot. Most important of all, the horse and rider need to stay relaxed and the horse should move freely forward. Once this is established a few lengthened strides can be attempted: ride into the corner in a slightly shortened working trot, make sure the horse is straight on the long side, make both legs firmer on the girth (using an even, forwards-driving leg and seat), move the hand slightly forward and let the horse move forwards energetically with longer strides. The horse should not be allowed to run – this is obvious; as the rhythm will get faster. Be patient! Lengthened and medium trot is difficult at first, even for those horses that have a natural talent.

Young horses need to first learn how to balance themselves. The movement of the back in medium trot is an energetic forward moving wave that has to be supported by the rider. Ideally this should be done in rising trot that is better for the young horse's back.

The rider must not tense her back or pelvis as it would interfere with the horse's movement.

Canter

The canter has three beats and is either left or right canter. In right canter, the horse starts with the left hind, followed by the diagonal pair right hind and left fore, followed finally by the right fore with a moment of suspension at the end, making it also a pace with impulsion. In canter too there is a working, medium and extended pace, although initially only working canter is asked for. The rest come later.

Once the young horse has learned the aids for canter (initially from trot), it should develop a canter with a soft; even contact in an energetic forward-going manner with a clear three-beat rhythm. Since it is much easier for the rider to sit in the saddle, compared to the trot, there are fewer problems in this area.

It is also easier for the young horse to find its balance in the canter. Like riding a bicycle, it is easier to go fast: going slow is much harder. Problems, though, can quickly

It is possible clearly to count the three beats of the canter: 1-2-3, 1-2-3. If instead you count a one, two-oo, three the rhythm is lost. The diagonal pair aren't landing at the same time. In this case you must ride strongly forward.

occur with turns and corners. Many young horses will change behind in an attempt to keep their balance: by doing this they support themselves with the outside hind. The rider must ride very rounded corners and on the circle keep a strong contact in the outside rein, almost as if wanting to ride the horse straight. This helps the horse to put the inside hind more under its body and stay in balance.

An extremely good exercise for a young horse is to go out for a canter (shorten your stirrups by at least two holes!) in a controlled but forward–going manner. The horse should be ridden in a deeper outline, in other words it should have its head and nose lower than when schooling at home, allowing it to round its back more. This allows its hindquarter to swing underneath more and helps it to keep its balance easier. You should only attempt this in open spaces, though, once the young horse is well established at home in the school. A bolting horse across county is far too dangerous! These first attempts should always be in the company of an experienced older horse.

The rider must not tense her back or pelvis as it would interfere with the horse's movement.

Freedom of paces

Although self explanatory, freedom of paces is also used to indicate the horse's ability to cover the ground in the individual paces. The ability of all of the joints of the horse's legs, including the shoulders and hips, to move freely must not be restricted. Freedom of paces is the result of relaxedness and rhythm. There are no special exercises to develop this element specifically, as only sensitive riding will achieve this unless of course the horse is either ill or in pain. If this is the case, consult a veterinarian or physiotherapist.

A good contact looks like this.

The horse will be in self-carriage (check by giving and retaking the reins) between the hand and the leg.

How to get the right contact

The correct contact is achieved at the moment when the horse is ridden forwards, from behind into the bridle. Because the rider is constantly encouraging the horse softly forward, moving in a relaxed and rhythmical

Contact

Usually a young horse will take up a contact very quickly, establishing the first connection with the rider's hand. This is an invaluable gift. To fiddle about now with heavy hands, or throw the reins away out of caution, will lose the horse's trust. Contact means having a connection. The right contact gives a horse the security to move in a relaxed and rhythmical way, in balance under the rider's weight.

In the ideal picture of a correct contact, the poll is the highest point (except when stretching), the nose is slightly in front of the vertical and the mouth will be relaxed and wet.

Imagine that you are leaning back against a door frame and suddenly it gives way or falls on top of you. Naturally you are only going to do this again with great hesitancy or even fear. A horse feels exactly the same if it is seeking a constant and even contact with the bit, looking as it is for the rider's hand.

Incorrect contact:

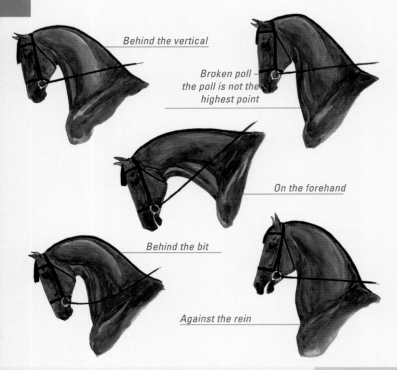

Behind the vertical

Broken poll – the poll is not the highest point

On the forehand

Behind the bit

Against the rein

short it will resist. The result will show in tenseness (pacing in the trot or a four–beat canter, for example) and irregularity in the paces. To rectify these problems you need to go back to working on rhythm and relaxedness by lungeing, pole work, encouraging the horse to stretch down, changing the reins frequently with lots of transitions – checking frequently by letting the horse take the rein down. In all of this work, a good forward-going tempo should be encouraged.

way, the horse rounds its back and stretches down onto the bit. This is a sign that the horse is ready to work with the rider, and needs to be reproduced every day for the horse's entire life.

A contact should never be forced. Hard, ungiving hands that work backwards always produce the wrong type of contact.

If the rider is incapable of keeping his hands steady, is lacking in feeling and sensitivity, or hasn't an independent elastic seat, then this will also result in the wrong type of contact. The horse won't be relaxed through the poll, it will tense the neck and back muscles – in

On the aids

If a horse steps up to the bit and stays in constant contact with the hand, it is standing "on the bit". That does not necessarily mean that it is also on the aids. The aids that are available to the rider to let the horse understand

The horse is on the bit..

what is wanted are as follows:

- *Weight or seat:* this may be used on both sides, one-sided or not used at all.
- *Legs:* used to drive forwards, forwards-sideways or supporting.
- *Reins:* the hands may be active giving, taking, yielding, blocking, supporting and directional.

Only when the aids are used together with a correct, relaxed and balanced seat is it possible to achieve harmony between horse and rider in all paces and movements.

The first principle is always that pushing or driving aids (seat and legs) are more important than restraining aids (rein or hand).

Weight aids

In the case of weight aids, i.e. the seat, used simultaneously **on both sides** the leg should lie on the girth line. Both seat bones will be exerting pressure forwards and downwards towards the knee and heel. The upper body stays upright and the stomach muscles are tightened. This is called "bracing the back".

This isn't a constant aid, but rather is used just for a moment. Bracing the back is a signal for the horse's hindquarters to become more active. Depending on how energetically this aid is given in conjunction with a giving rein aid, the horse will walk from halt, trot from walk or even trot from the halt.

A *one-sided weight aid* is used when the horse is flexed or positioned to the inside when cantering, and as a prerequisite for a change of direction.

The best way to feel what is meant by "bracing your back" is to sit on the edge of a drum or box that comes half-way up your upper thigh. Your feet should be placed as far apart as the width of a horse's chest, with the heels resting on the ground and the upper body held upright. You should be mimicking your riding position. You should now try to tip the barrel forward; in doing so, you will unintentionally be using the right muscles while transferring your weight towards your knee and heel.

Once you are aware of how you have done it, you will know how to engage your seat by "bracing your back" and should be able to replicate this in the saddle. You will also realise that to engage your seat like this, the legs play a vital part – otherwise the drum tips over on-to you!

If you can also vary the intensity or strength of bracing your back, then you have learnt the key to good riding. This is crucial in the correct usage of the half-halt and the horse will quickly learn to react to this.

If, for example, you want the horse to turn to the right, the right seat bone should be pushed forwards and downwards while the hips remain braced. Your torso should always be stretched tall and you should avoid collapsing through the hip. This aid is also a prerequisite for leg and rein aids.

The forwards driving leg on the girth.

The forwards-sideways driving leg a hand's breadth behind the girth.

A *lighter* seat is used when the horse's back and hindquarters need to be relieved of weight, resulting in the horse being able to move more freely. The seat remains in the saddle but the weight goes more onto the thigh and knee, while the upper body leans slightly forward. This aid is useful when training young horses, warming up, riding up gentle slopes and for the first attempts at reining back.

Leg aids

The forward driving leg aid drives the horse forward in all paces, with the rider's leg just behind the girth applying a gentle pressure on both sides.

The forwards-sidewards driving leg aid is used in lateral work, including leg yielding, whereby the rider's lower leg lies a hand's breadth behind the girth. The knee and heel should not be drawn up. The forwards-side-ways leg aid supports the one-sided engage-ment of the rider's seat.

The supporting leg aid is used as a bal-ance opposite the forwards or forwards-sidewards driving aid by preventing the hindquarters from falling out. The supporting leg is also placed about a hand's breadth behind the girth but is not as active.

Rein aids

The rein aids (in other words the hand) are never used alone. Only a horse that is work-ing through allows the rein aids to work from the mouth over the poll, down the neck and back into the hindquarters. The horse lets the aids through, in other words it accepts the hand and is submissive to the aid.

With the *active* (erroneously called "tak-ing") rein aid, the hand is closed more firm-ly or slightly turned to the inside in order to shorten the rein a little – in both cases only for a moment. Pulling on the reins is a mortal sin!

An active hand is always followed by a *yielding* hand. The fists return to their usual position with relaxed fingers. This does not mean that the contact to the horse's mouth should be broken; it should always be there, even with the yielding rein aid.

Blocking rein aids are used when the horse goes against the hand or above the reins. The hands are in their usual position, the back is braced and the legs are actively driving forward. The pressure that results from this must be held until the horse gives in to the rider, accepts the bit and becomes lighter in the hand. This moment must not be missed, as the hands must immediately become softer and the seat relaxed as a reward to the horse! This way the horse will better understand what we want from it.

Directional rein aids are used when the horse is to move along a curved line, for example a circle. On the left rein, the left hand is moved across inwards very slightly so that the horse's left eye and nostril are just visible. On the right hand of course the opposite happens.

The directional aid is always given with the *supporting* aid that helps to maintain the curve. Thus on the left rein the supporting rein would be the right hand. These aids are always given with the one-sided active leg aid and the one-sided weight aid.

A sideways leading rein aid will particularly help young horses in the direction of the bend. This is also useful when teaching lateral movements.

On a long rein the rider should still have a contact to the horse's mouth but the horse should go in a more natural outline, with the head lowered and the neck stretched.

On a completely loose rein the rider lets the reins out to the buckle. There is no contact with the horse's mouth and the horse has a lowered head and neck.

Accompanied by the relevant weight aid, the hand is moved away from the horse's neck and over slightly in the direction of the intended movement. Once the horse has accepted this aid the other hand should give to follow the active hand.

Rein aids are never to be used in isolation. The hand alone cannot force the horse to give at the poll.

Half-halt

All aids (leg, seat and hands) are used at the same time for the half-halt. The rider puts more weight into the seat, braces the back, closes the leg and restricts the horse from taking off in front with a restraining hand. The rider is in effect pushing the horse together from the back to the front and immediately follows with a giving hand or rein.

Giving and retaking the reins should last 3–4 seconds.

A half-halt is not a single action, but follows the rhythm of the movement.
It is used:
* *to make transitions from one pace to another*
* *to regulate the tempo within a pace*
* *to prepare the horse for some sort of change, for example of pace, movement, etc.*
* *to create, keep and improve the contact and later to collect the horse*
* *overall to ride the horse correctly.*

Giving and retaking the reins

Giving and retaking the reins is a test of a horse's self-carriage and shows whether the horse is working between the leg and the seat. To do this the rider moves both hands forwards up the neck for two to three strides. The hands are then quietly moved back to the original position. This exercise can be done in all paces.

The half-halt is a brief impulse given from a well balanced seat.

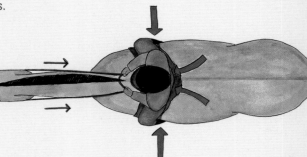

The halt

The halt is only asked for on a straight line and can occur from any pace, although when starting out it should only be done from the walk and trot. A strong half-halt leads to a halt! A more active seat and legs will push the horse into a blocking hand that yields to become soft just before the horse comes to a halt. Young horses use their necks as a counterbalance when coming in to a halt. Stepping back and forth, standing with their legs apart and nodding with the head are all considered major faults. The latter indicates a heavy hand.

Don't forget to give with the hand when halting.

Straightness

If most of us are right-handed, then most horses are right-footed, with the right hind being stronger than the left. Most horses shy to the left when they are spooked, and spooks on the right are usually the ones that they see first!

Many young horses find turning (not flexing!) to the left easier, as the more powerful right hind acts as a support. For this reason, lungeing or any working-in should be started on the left rein. It is for this reason that vaulting and equine circus performances are always carried out on the left rein as well.

In the first months of training you will have to live with this natural crookedness. Until the horse is on the aids, however, you will not be able to straighten it without resistance and tension. Most horses are hollow to the right, leading the rider to believe that this is the better side. In reality it is the worse side, because the horse will be tensing all of the muscles on the right side. The result is that

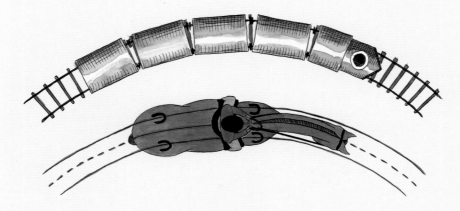

The straightened horse should move as if on a railway track with the back hooves following in the tracks of the front.

it will be leaning on the left shoulder and won't accept the right rein. A horse can be said to be straight when it moves on one track with the hind feet following the front feet on straight as well as curved lines.

It is easy to check whether the horse is moving absolutely straight by riding on a freshly harrowed surface: the tracks left behind will tell you if there is a problem. Only when the horse is straight can the impulsion from the hindquarters really be harnessed. Straightening the horse also means improving its balance, because both halves of the body will then be subjected to the same amount of weight and exertion. In the long term this will help to protect its legs.

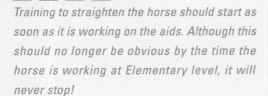

Training to straighten the horse should start as soon as it is working on the aids. Although this should no longer be obvious by the time the horse is working at Elementary level, it will never stop!

How to achieve straightness

The basic rule is that the forehand is always reliant on the hindquarters. This means that any adjustments should be made to the forehand, rather than adjusting the quarters to the front. Start by riding circles, serpentines, changes of rein diagonally across the school and larger voltes. It is very important that these figures are ridden correctly otherwise there is no value in doing them! Don't work the horse on its "bad" side too long, as this may be too much for it and can lead to sore muscles and reluctance to work at all. Always try to take the relaxedness and rhythm from the "good" to the "bad" side. Change the rein often, and also do lots of transitions within the pace, as this helps to move the horse forward onto a soft contact.

Serpentines

Serpentines across the school (loops touching both long sides) usually start with three or four loops but can be done with five later. The loops begin and end in the middle of the short side. A serpentine of three loops, for example, can start with a half circle at A, rounding it off, straightening the horse for a few strides, changing the bend and riding the next half circle, touching the long side of the school at B. There is then another straight line and a half circle to bring the horse to C.

The following corner also needs to be ridden correctly as well. The purpose of serpentines is to test the willingness of the horse to change the bend and straighten between the bends.

Serpentines on the long side are a bit more difficult and can be ridden with single or double loops. A single loop serpentine is ridden to a depth of five metres out from the track (i.e. a quarter of the school's width). After correctly riding the corner, the horse is bent to the inside and is moving away from the track. After about two horse lengths, the bend is changed so that the outside leg now becomes the inside leg. The furthest point out from the track is reached opposite E/B at five metres from the track and on reaching this point you start to return to the track, again changing the bend about two horse lengths out from the track, meeting the track at H or F.

In the two-loop serpentines everything happens a bit faster. The furthest the horse moves away from the track is two and a half metres, and in the middle the horse returns to the track at E or B, meaning the changes of bend happen fairly quickly. The rider must be confident in giving the correct aids and the horse must be supple and relaxed. Any stiffness from either horse or rider will be noticed immediately, making this exercise an ideal test of a rider's independent seat and

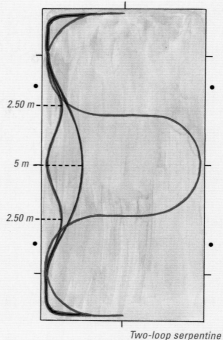

2.50 m

5 m

2.50 m

Two-loop serpentine ——
One-loop serpentine ——
Serpentine across the school, three loops ——

soft hands, and the horse's obedience and suppleness.

Riding turns

The most important principle in riding turns is that the fore and hind legs should follow behind one other, as if on a railway track. This means that the bend must go through the whole of the horse's body, and not just through the neck.

Corners, voltes and half-circles

The *volte* demands the greatest degree of flexion from a horse. The smallest volte a horse can perform without moving on two tracks is one six metres in diameter. It is for this reason that voltes are usually ridden with a diameter of ten metres when training begins, while more advanced work demands eight-metre circles. The corners of the school in effect require a quarter of a ten-metre volte, but initially this is rounded out somewhat, and as the training progresses it will be possible to ride deeper into the corner. The volte is round, and ends where it begins. The horse should move along the same track with good rhythm and impulsion, the aids similar to when riding a corner.

Patience and sensitivity are required by the rider to complete a correct volte; if the inside rein is too heavy, the inside leg too strong or the outside leg too weak the horse will be pulled around or the hindquarters will fall out.

The *half circle with a change of rein*, often ridden out of the corner, is ridden like a volte for the first half. At the half-way point (widest point) though the horse will be straightened and ridden back to the track diagonally.

Leg Yielding

Leg yielding is an important and useful exercise at the beginning of a horse's dressage training. Later, though, it is not advisable when developing collection and extension, as the horse is asked to move away from the leg instead of becoming engaged and it goes against the principle of adjusting the forehand to the haunches. At the start of the straightening work though it is very useful for both horse and rider in developing a feel for the use of the correct lateral aids.

Leg yielding should help develop a horse's submission and prepare it for the lateral aids. The rider's inside leg pushes the horse more into the outside hand and the horse moves forwards and sideways on two tracks slightly flexed but without bending.

The horse should move twice as far forwards as it does sideways, with the inside fore and hind feet moving evenly forwards and over the outside feet. The horse is always flexed to the side of the rider's driving leg.

—— a: Volte and b: Corner
—— a: half circle with a change of rein and b: in the corner

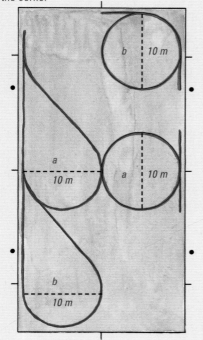

b | 10 m

a
10 m

a | 10 m

b
10 m

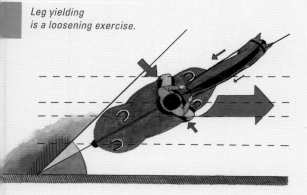

*Leg yielding
is a loosening exercise.*

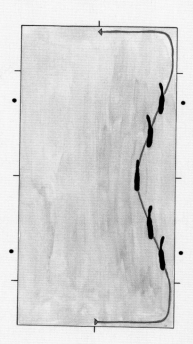

The rider needs to put more weight on the inside seat bone, with the inside leg lying just behind the girth and driving forwards and sideways, while the outside leg supports just behind the girth, preventing the hindquarters dropping out and keeping the forward movement. The inside rein creates a slight flexion and the outside rein prevents too large a bend and keeps the shoulder from falling out.

*This is a good exercise to check
if the horse is on the aids.*

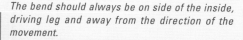

The bend should always be on side of the inside, driving leg and away from the direction of the movement.

Leg yielding exercises

Leg yielding to the five metre line and back to the track is ridden like any leg yield, only the horse is moving diagonally away from and back to the track. It should make the horse more obedient to the forwards-sideways driving leg and the leading, containing outside rein.

After the corner the rider should flex the horse slightly to the outside and push with what is now the new inside leg (previously outside) forwards and sideways diagonally across the school. The horse should stay parallel to the sides of the school and the hindquarters must not step further over than the forehand. Once level with the line between E and B, horse and rider should be five metres out from the track, the horse is straightened for a horse length and then changed to the other bend and ridden back in the same way to the track.

Many mistakes can be made when leg yielding, making the exercise useless. The *rider* may be tense, twist his body or collapse a hip. He may not put his weight on the inside seat bone correctly, or put his inside leg too far back, not feeling when he should be pushing and when not. Often the outside leg is not positioned correctly and the forwards movement is lost. Mainly, though, the inside rein is used too strongly, pulling the horse's neck round and enabling it to escape out through the outside shoulder. If any or all of this happens, the whole exercise will end in chaos. The *horse* in turn may grind its teeth, tilt its head or neck, go against the bit resulting in a change of tempo and possibly falling out through the shoulder. The hind legs may not cross over, or the quarters may trail to the outside. In other words, leg yielding should only be used when the rider's seat and aids are secure enough and the horse itself is securely on the aids. Otherwise leg yielding will do more harm than good.

Balance

Without a rider, a horse moves in balance without any problems whatsoever. Once it has a rider on its back it has to find its balance all over again. The prerequisite for lateral balance is straightness. A horse that is straight, can be turned easily with minimal aids and moves in parallel, as if on railway track, and is laterally balanced. This can be checked by the rider holding the reins in one hand while riding on straight and curved lines. The contact must always be maintained and the horse must remain on the tracks! This exercise once formed a part of dressage tests in Germany, but was taken out some years ago.

It is worthwhile trying to ride with one hand, but please stay relaxed! This exercise is also a very good for your seat.

than carrying. Now it is time for the back legs to be made to step under the horse more, moving the centre of gravity back, thus taking more weight off the body and lightening the forehand. This raising of the forehand is helped by the frequent use of half-halts before correctly ridden corners and by the use of halting from trot and canter. Tempo variations within the trot and canter also help to push the horse through from behind.

Medium trot and medium canter

The reason why lateral balance is so important to a horse can be easily seen by comparing it to a bicycle. It is easy to ride without hands on a well balanced bike, but if it isn't upright and balanced then you will need your arms as a balancing pole and your upper body as a counter-balance. If a horse permanently leans to the left, the rider will hang on to the left rein (ending up with a sore arm), or more frequently will collapse the left hip. While bicycles can be sent for repair, the only thing that can help the horse is patient and persistent daily use of all of the exercises that will develop straightness and suppleness on both sides.

So far, our attention has been concentrated on the relaxation and stretching of the horse's muscles in order to achieve a rounded and swinging back. The horse has been allowed to stretch forwards and downwards without us worrying that the horse has been moving more or less on the forehand, with the hindquarters pushing more rather

Whether riding an extended pace out of trot or canter, the method is the same and is usually done on a straight line. Both though can be ridden on a circle in order to encourage the inside hind leg to move through better. In order to ride a long side in medium trot or canter, both corners of the short side before should be used to get the horse to engage its quarters more. The outside leg prevents the haunches falling out and a half halt prepares the horse.

After the corner leading into the long side, the horse should be straightened and the impulsion that has been created on the short side should be released, using even driving aids. The hands should move a little forward so that the horse is able to put its nose slightly in front of the vertical and take longer strides by pushing through from behind. It should lengthen its frame but the rhythm should not become faster – if anything it should become slower because the moment of suspension is longer. To go back to the

In medium trot the horse's frame will become longer.

In collected trot the frame is shortened.

In the transition from medium to working or collected canter it is important that you sit exactly as you would when going into canter, otherwise the horse may drop back into trot.

Reducing and enlarging the circle is also a good exercise to engage the hocks more.

Gymnastic jumping, which can be more demanding than at the start of training, and hacking out on hills also help develop the horse's balance.

The result of this is, as mentioned above, the raising of the forehand, with the hindquarters carrying more weight and the forehand becoming lighter. The horse will move more elegantly and appear to go uphill – all the result of conscientious and correct work.

When are you both ready for a double bridle?

A *rider* is ready to ride with a double bridle when he is able to co-ordinate all the aids competently.

The most important factor of all; though, is sensitive hands that are independent of the body. The rider should be able to competently ride all of the movements of an Elementary test.

The *horse* must work softly and lightly through the poll and of course work on the aids. It should be comfortable with all of the movements at an Elementary level (including the start of collection). Ideally the horse should be able to be ridden in a snaffle bridle at the highest level, and should be

working pace, half-halts should be given two to three horse lengths before the required point. The aids are given more strongly and the horse is pushed together again until the desired tempo (working or collected) is reached.

able to change from a double bridle to a snaffle with ease.

If someone claims that their horse "only goes well in a double bridle" then you can be sure that there is something wrong with the training.

Nothing can be achieved in a double bridle that you can't do in a plain snaffle.

When riding with a double bridle the bridoon (snaffle bit) should always take precedence or, in other words, be used for the main contact. The curb bit should be used to refine the aid. If the curb is held too strongly the horse will tilt its head, especially in turns. If the rider carries his hands too high, the horse will become too narrow through the neck, thanks to the levering action.

If a horse is working in a double bridle correctly and in collection then it will naturally work onto the curb, which can then be used for fine adjustments.

Collection can never be forced with a double bridle. This always causes a hollowing of the back that reduces the amount of weight carried through the hindquarters and lessens the engagement of the hocks.

Submission

Submission means that there is a constant contact between the hindquarters and the rider's hand through which energy can flow. Signals from the hand are sent back to influence the hindquarters without resistance. There should be no resistance in the mouth or through the poll, and the horse should accept all the aids.

How is submission encouraged?

This quality is developed by the ever finer use of the half-halt and halt. The transitions from canter to trot and from trot to walk help not only to slow the horse down, but also to bring the hocks more under the horse and onto the bit. The rider pushes the horse forwards from the three-beat rhythm of the canter to the two beats of the trot, from the two-beat rhythm of the trot to the four beats of the walk. This also applies to transitions into a square halt. The horse must accept all of the aids without tension in order to come to a balanced halt with its hocks well underneath it. The weight of both the rider and horse will then be evenly spread over all four legs. The best test of this is rein back immediately after halting. If you can then trot or canter on maintaining rhythm and softness, then you can be certain that your horse is working through correctly.

Impulsion

Impulsion and submission are inseparable. Impulsion is the powerful thrust from the hindquarters propelling the horse forwards and travelling through an elastic, swinging back and a relaxed neck. Impulsion should not be confused with the natural paces. The paces are the horse's natural ability to move at different speeds. Impulsion is the result of training by the rider, and although the natural paces of the horse are used, the rider

A horse moving with impulsion swings through in the back and allows the rider to sit easily. It should not be hurried.

works on achieving relaxedness, thrust from the hindquarters and submission. As with all the other elements of the training tree, here too is the soft, elastic seat and the correct aids from the rider of greatest importance. For the horse, the prerequisite is that all the previous stages have been worked through and are well established.

A horse moving with impulsion bends the hock immediately forwards (not upwards or even backwards) after pushing off from it. As a result of the forward thrust and the horse's swinging back, the rider is in effect pushed into the horse, leading to a deeper seat. The trot and canter extensions become more ground-covering, the action of the front legs will improve and the moment of suspension will become longer.

How is impulsion encouraged?

Impulsion is worked on in exactly the same way as submission. If the horse is balanced and submissive, then it should also show impulsion. Increased but soft pressure from the leg and seat together with an elastic and giving hand that won't restrict the stepping through of the hocks will help to develop impulsion.

If there is irregularity in the rhythm, tense strides, or if the horse gets hurried and runs; then there is something wrong.

If there is no lengthening of the horse's frame, the horse goes on the forehand or must balance itself by stepping wide behind, then the mistake will be in the earlier training.

Collection

"True collection" "

A horse is not born with collected paces. No horse would move for any length of time in a collected trot in the wild. Nearly every horse can learn dressage movements; however, not every horse is a dressage horse. Whether a horse is capable of collection or not will depend on its conformation and mental attitude. Experience, knowledge and sensitivity are also demanded of the rider. A perfectly collected horse is not the aim of basic training, but is of more interest to the dressage specialist. At Elementary level, only the beginnings of the signs of collection should be asked for.

Collection means the development of the horse's ability to carry itself. The centre of gravity is shifted further back, with the croup lowering and the hocks engaged and carrying more weight. At the same time the forehand will become lighter and raised. The horse's frame will become shorter and the horse will appear to go uphill. This elevation, or raising of the forehand must always be in relation to the lowering of the hindquarters for it to be a true collection.

This can only be achieved when all the other elements of training are well established. In collection, the horse also needs to move freely with a swinging back, and the paces must remain even and true. Walk, trot and canter will become shorter and more impressive, showing more elevation and cadence. The whole picture of horse and rider should be harmonious. The double bridle is not a tool to force collection, but should be

"False collection"

used to refine the aids. If the prerequisites for collection are missing, then a double bridle won't help and can in fact do more harm than good – the result being a "false collection". This type of collection is forced by the hand and the leverage of the bit. The horse will not be able to carry itself and will instead pull the head and neck up and back. Its back will hollow and its legs will push out behind instead of underneath. There is nothing resembling collection in sight!

The beginnings of collection can be achieved by using tempo changes within the trot and canter, ensuring that the rhythm and

Reining back is a good exercise for collection. The sequence of steps is the same as in the trot. Immediately trotting on from the rein back increases the collecting effect.

Moving in collection is hard work for the horse. That's why we should not demand increased engagement for too long at any one time. There should always be regular breaks for stretching and relaxing in between. Think of the horse as a spring– you can only press it together for a short time, then you have to let go and the spring uncoils. The horse is exactly the same – after a collecting exercise the impulsion needs to be let out forwards, by riding medium trot or canter. If the paces become uneven then it is a sign that the collection wasn't yet right and further work still needs to be done on submission and impulsion before trying to collect again. To continue working when the collection is not right or working too long on it leads to tension and resistance. Letting the horse take the bit down and stretch is always a reward after hard work.

Collection can't be held for ever – you have to let go sometime.

impulsion aren't lost. Halting from trot, rein backs and trotting from halt are all good exercises. Cantering from walk, decreasing and increasing circles and eight-metre voltes in canter will all gradually encourage greater collection. If these can all be done without any difficulty, then collection will follow. Simple changes and half pirouettes will become easier, just as counter canter can only be worked on once collection is started.

This should be your horse's reward: its back rounds up, its neck lowers until its nose is even with the point of the shoulder.

Concluding comments

Once a stage is reached when the horse trusts the rider enough to work in a relaxed, rhythmical and forward-going manner on a secure contact with the first signs of collection: whether at home, out hacking and over small jumps, then basic training is completed.

To reach this point takes two to two-and-a-half years: to do it more quickly could cost you the horse's health. It takes time to build up muscles as well as the mental ability of the horse to want to work with the rider.

After at least two years of careful and systematic work a horse will be ready for further training in a specialised discipline, whether this be dressage, jumping or eventing. During its basic training a horse will have already shown which of these it has a talent for and to which it is best suited. So many horses are bought as a dressage prospect but end up as jumping successes, and vice versa. What ever the case, basic training applies to all if they want to achieve success in their chosen discipline.

The first elements of the training tree are so important that without them, even hacking out will be no fun for either horse or rider! Relaxedness, rhythm, freedom of paces and contact in the first development phase, are all the basis of any further activity in the saddle. These four points overlap each other so much that you can't separate them out: one depends on the other. Von Ziegner refers to these elements as Phase A.

A horse that is working well in the first four elements of training will go like this out hacking...

: ... and not like this!

Phase B overlaps Phase A and builds on it. Contact must exist for the horse to be able to work on the aids. Only then can it be straightened and balanced.

Phase A: Familiarisation

Phase B: On the aids

Phase C: Collection

cises, out of which rhythm and freedom of paces result, with the horse seeking a contact from the rider's hand. For horses whose basic training is completed , this will all happen simultaneously.

It is not sensible to demand "the whole programme" every day from your horse; any horse, even the keenest, will soon lose interest. A sensitive rider sometimes will only concentrate on the elements of Phase A. Perhaps the day before the horse was worked horse particularly hard? Perhaps the rider is not one hundred per cent fit, in which case it is better to ride well for a short time, rather than working longer, but badly.

Hacking out, if weather and ground permit, lungeing or loose schooling over jumps are sometimes the better option.

A rider who trains his own horse will forge a special bond with it. This rider will want to keep his horse healthy and sound for as long as possible so that he has full enjoyment from the results of this work.

"I love my horse and take plenty of time and patience training it correctly. I would always be grateful for expert help and advice!"

The foundation for Phase C in turn is a balanced horse in order to be able to work on submission, leading in turn to impulsion that inevitably results in collection.

Every day, the steps of the training tree should be repeated in miniature. Any training session should begin with stretching exer-